Stained Glass is the 1993 Lamon
of The Academy of American Poets.

From 1954 through 1974 the Lamont Poetry Selection
supported the publication and distribution of a first collection
of poems. Since 1975 this distinguished award has been given
for an American poet's second book.

Judges for 1993: Amy Clampitt, Jorie Graham, Richard Kenney.

STAINED
GLASS

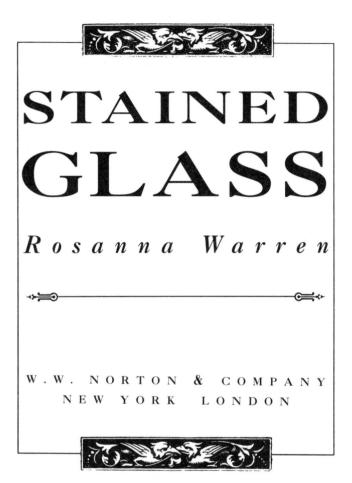

STAINED GLASS

GLASS

Rosanna Warren

W.W. NORTON & COMPANY
NEW YORK LONDON

The text of this book is composed in Simoncini Garamond,
with the display set in Caslon Roman.
Composition by PennSet, Inc.
Manufacturing by The Courier Companies, Inc.
Book design by Guenet Abraham.

Library of Congress Cataloging-in-Publication Data

Warren, Rosanna.
  Stained glass / Rosanna Warren.
    p. cm.
  I. Title.
  PS3573.A7793S7 1993
  811'.54—dc20   92-37194

ISBN 0-393-03486-0

W. W. Norton & Company, Inc., 500 Fifth Avenue, New York, N.Y. 10110

W. W. Norton & Company Ltd., 10 Coptic Street, London WC1A 1PU

1 2 3 4 5 6 7 8 9 0

ACKNOWLEDGMENTS

Grateful acknowledgment is made to the following journals in which these poems have appeared:

American Poetry Review: "Same Taste," "Verso," "Love in the Shop" (translations from Pierre Reverdy)

Agni: "Science Lessons"

The Anthology of New England Writers: "In Creve Coeur, Missouri"

Arion: "A Garland from Alcman"

The Atlantic Monthly: "Season Due," "Necrophiliac" (original title "Elegist"), "Song"

The Boston Phoenix: "From New Hampshire," "Mountain View"

Boulevard: "The Cormorant," "Farm," "Umbilical"

Chelsea: "His Long Home" (original title "With You")

The Georgia Review: "Two days before"

Grand Street: "Le Ventre de Paris: A Marriage Poem"

The New Republic: "The Cost"

The New Yorker: "Man, that is Born of a Woman"

Partisan Review: "Christ at the Movies" (translation of Max Jacob)

Ploughshares: "Ice," "Daily Mail"

Seneca Review: "Infernal Vision in the Form of a Madrigal," "Agonies and More" (translations from Max Jacob);" Hagar," "Lena's House," "The Broken Pot,""An Old Cubist"

The Southwest Review: "Child Model," "Tide Pickers"

Verse: "Eskimo Widow"

Western Humanities Review: "Pornography"

The Yale Review: "Girl by Minoan Wall," "Jacob Burckhardt, August 8, 1897," "The Twelfth Day"

The poem "Alcman" first appeared in the chapbook "A Garland for John Hollander."

"The Cormorant" appeared in *The Best American Poetry 1990,* edited by Jorie Graham, Series Editor, David Lehman, Collier Books.

"Song" appeared in *The Best American Poetry 1991*, edited by Mark Strand, Series Editor, David Lehman, Collier Books.

"Necrophiliac" appeared in *The Best American Poetry 1992*, edited by Charles Simic, Series Editor, David Lehman, Collier Books.

Max Jacob's poem "Christ at the Movies" (*"Le Christ au cinematographe"*), from his volume *La Defense de Tartufe* (Gallimard, 1964); "Agonies and More" (*"Angoisses et autres"*), from *Fond de l'eau* (1927); and "Infernal Vision in the Form of a Madrigal" (*"Vision infernale en forme de madrigal"*), from *Les Penitents en Maillots Roses* (1925), are all reprinted courtesy of Editions Gallimard.

Pierre Reverdy's poems "Verso" (from *Cravates de chanvre*, 1922), "Same Taste" (*"Saveur pareille"*), and "Love in the Shop" (*"L'Amour dans la boutique"*), from *La Guitare endormie* (1919), are reprinted courtesy of Editions Flammarion.

I am grateful as well to the Robert Frost Farm in Franconia, New Hampshire, and to Katherine and Tony Jackson, for the refuges they provided.

FOR MY MOTHER
AND IN MEMORY OF MY FATHER

CONTENTS

I

II

III

IV

And made Hell grant what Love did seek
—Milton, "Il Penseroso"

SEASON DUE

They are unforgiving and do not ask mercy, these last
of the season's flowers: chrysanthemums, brash
marigolds, fat sultan dahlias a-nod

    in rain. It is
    September. Pansy
    freaked with jet be

damned: it takes this radiant bitterness to
stand, to take the throb of sky, now sky
is cold, falls bodily, assaults. In tangled

    conclave, spiky-
    leaved, they
    wait. The news

is fatal. Leaf by leaf, petal
by petal, they brazen out this chill
which has felled already gentler flowers and herbs

    and now probes
    these veins for a last
    mortal volley of

cadmium orange, magenta, a last acrid flood
of perfume that will drift in the air here once more,
yet once more, when these stubborn flowers have died.

Hagar

And the water was spent in the bottle, and she cast the child under one of the shrubs. (Gen. 21:15)

Was it a mountain wavering on the rim
of sky, or only air, shaken like a flame?
Dust stung my nostrils. Lizards fled
over the sharp track where my feet had bled.
My sandal thongs were broken. The water was gone.
I cracked the jar, it cracked like an old bone.
Lord of the desert, did you bless
that birth? Bonded to Abraham, did I guess
his wilderness? He thrust
us out from the squandering of his lust
after I'd framed its future. Hers as well,
griping mistress whose belly would not swell,
witch whose hair I brushed and wound in braids,
whose robe I stitched, whose veil I decked with beads
to snag his pleasure. What was left my own?
Not my bought body, surely. Not my son.
Only that core of shock from which he surged,
the spasm that unbonded me, and purged
me of Master and Mistress and the Lord.
I pressed my knees to the rock, and poured
my body out like sand across the sand.
Not to see him die, I pressed my hand
into my sockets, but his cry broke through
all bone and fiber, shattered the sealed blue
of heaven to wound your vast and hovering ear,
Lord of the desert, Lord who cannot hear
our prayers, but the deathwail of a child
startling from the rootclutch in the wild.

You are the God of stone and stony eyes
and water dripping through stone crevices
to the swollen tongue that cannot taste your name.
Lord of thistle and mica. Here I am.

LE VENTRE DE PARIS:
A MARRIAGE POEM

I

La Rue Montorgeuil: the Market

They built the church here, imagining
He would come
to these cobbles, these streaming gutters,
the white pig's head skinned with drowsing eyes;
He would finger
dahlia petals mashed in the sewer,
chicken clutch, eel coil, choirs
of shrimp;
He would touch you, touch
me, because we are equally
soiled, because butchery
is life, and life runs
in us as down this street.

II

St. Eustache: the Market Church

The little we know
of St. Eustache
becomes him: how
this Roman (third
century A.D.) general

while hunting beheld
a crucifix
in a stag's antlers
and instantly
converted; how

broiled
in an iron bull, his cries
converted
to music; how, trans-
lated, he blesses

this butchers' cathedral,
its stained glass, its *clochards*,
its organ recitals,
its street
whistling with market blood.

Eskimo widow

She sees nothing, her eyes are closed.
I see her lying face down, cheek smooth
on rocks worn smooth by tides.
I hear what she hears: kayaks

stitching wave folds,
rustle and slap. I see, she doesn't,
the surprised mouth each paddle scoops
in water, for the autumn migration.

They don't take her. They won't:
blood oozing out all down the path
where she crawled, begging.
The last child she lost. No man.

Blood on stone. Bad omen.
Her cries have drained out:
she can't hear herself now.
Nor can I hear

her: she's a story
draining. The kayaks prick
around the headland into open
sea, where I lose them

as I lose her
alone on the shore
where she shelters
in the dome of her own name.

CHILD MODEL

FOR ROSALIE CARLSON

(Greenland Eskimo mummy, boy, four years old,
National Geographic, February 1985)

I want to adopt you, doll-like child,
your death, your *National
Geographic* resurrection. Cold

has clasped you in its cache, all
gaze, all glimmer. Arctic star,
cuddled in sealskin grave-creche, still

you wait there for your mother,
trusting she'll trudge back through the snow,
famine, centuries: lift you from this glamour,

snatch you, full-limbed, laughing home. But now
in these pages, trapped, you touch
for comfort tiny beads of bone. We know

nothing of you save that such
patient beauty, still unputrefied,
was never seen in death. We clutch

you, ancient child: we need
to think you're saved, as if one face unmarred
in Kodachrome rescued all others who have died

ugly, bruised, disqualified.

ESKIMO MOTHER

I know what I have to do, a small thing.
And then he will want his stew blubber hacked
from the good fat seal.
Then he will want his stew.
A small thing. In my sealskin anorak

I will go down to the shore with the small
girl-child nestled to me, and will weight her swaddling
with four stones, each the size of my hand.
I know what I have to do,
I know: no good at paddling,

eats too much, can't hunt,
and we have enough hands to stretch and stitch the skins.
I know the warm wedge of her
under my breast, urgent gums
triggering the nipple, the happy

confident milk tugging me out
into her where we have no secrets.
How could he know, returning now
from a four-month hunt, sledge loaded
with seals, but not enough. How could he know

what I know, what my sister and cousin
know but won't say as they turn
from me, as I walk
the shore path in the late, iodine light,
my small thing tucked so carefully under my arm.

PORNOGRAPHY

That's good, the charcoal triangle of eye
as illegible, impenetrable, as the dark
furred cleft so laconically displayed
between belly swell and the soft sag of thigh;

good, the airbrushed, antiqued cerulean
of kimono and cloudlets (what's a kimono
doing on a rowboat, anyway?)
to tip us off to the Baudelairean

managerial style of this photographer
who revels, clearly, in correspondences.
O turtled, inky murk: swallow the skiff,
swallow the rug and cushion, engulf her

who lolls so improbably looking for trouble
among the cattails in glossy, pungent mud.
Sweet lard, folded, smeared and spread
for finger-sinking: as the fable

develops her, she will slide
into reflective ooze, sleazy
Ophelia, too milky, too azure here
with virgin eye, and cleft that never cried.

SCIENCE LESSONS

The human body is superfluous.
Rochester knew it: lurching home
from a night of swiving and sluicing,
ballocks crumpled, loins wrung out,
fingers dripping and pungent, he was consumed

by knowledge. Having caressed
the soft slippage of flesh from rib and hip,
foreknew rack, gibbet, kettle, all the precise
instruments of quest including
the final, eloquent shudder; knew

pond scum to grow gooseflesh, to be
as freakishly aroused; knew Spanish moss
to dangle as lace, black mud to suck
and ooze with a confession of pleasure;
knew truth a prisoner

begging to be shucked free.
So over and over the glossy girl,
the sleek-limbed boy, must pose
while Love the scientist stutters, repeats himself,
staggers through his garbled litanies

husking pure form from the body of this death.

Courtly love

Blank room, blank window, and his back bared
to us in a ganglion of shadow, hers
to him: love is a questing blade
of light across floorboards charred

by its progress. The woman stands
out of reach, anonymous shoulders sloped
nude above her drooping cape and gloved
hands on the sill. His gaze, invisible, bends

toward her who refuses. The vase
between them heralds
an annunciation: that they need
betweenness—sunshaft, blossom, falling caress

of cloak—as much as they need
our looking. Their charity
is their facelessness, their violence
immobility. So will they feed

and deprive forever the starved eye
whose pupil contracts
in a spasm of infinite
recession. Time to pay.

The cost

That wasn't our baby
in the trashcan in the city zoo
someone else picked it out someone
else wrapped it in paper and dropped it in

    Why do you sleep
    with your back to me

Besides it's another city we don't
live there anymore

    Because it's cold

Besides I collect
phrases these days not babies
spartan clasp   jute finish   crotch island

    Last winter was colder
    we lived by the Swedenborgian Institute
    where you had your accident

Or that list of words from the summer in Florence
the essential list warm clues
like *sausage   torture   bilge* I knew
I'd need the rest of my life

but I lost it

    The ice at the corner scared me

My hands soiled with news

    That wasn't our baby

Virginity   elocution   electrocution
light sliding off the ailanthus spikes

    It was another city

It was still breathing

The cost of empire is great and disturbing
the secret knowledge of philosophy

We weren't the ones

Tannin

Amor Fati was a nice girl
    but foreign
Like all of us she felt the tidal haul

    Menses and sacred discs
    of heart and solar plexus pull

Love   the unnatural stimulant

You gnashing the forest into syntax with the power saw
I hoarding my knowledge like a cyst
    as sweet gasoline fumes rise
      to the veranda
    and the lake shrivels

The singular procession fares on
with the sun blipping up to reveal
les causes secrètes de la Révolution du 9 Thermidor
in the pages of Carlyle

    Tannin and white pine
    sublimed to fear
    This is the taste

    of my etheric double
      not yet lost
    keening and whetting her tongue

on the whine of the saw   on the steel blade of air

II

GIRL BY MINOAN WALL

If, from a centuried window, she looks out
    toward a blinding swatch
of Aegean, it is toward
    a secret self, years
from now, who will stroll in the same sun

    over cobbles, who will peer
at blistered stucco and Turkish ogive
    windows, and wonder
what ghosts observe her, in what tongue
    they speak. And I

watching her, watch already
    a ghost. This solid
sun-browned girl, pad and pencil in lap, cheek
    on palm, already

burns. Her flesh, like the town wall, quavers
    in the heat-smite
of noon: by evening her very frame
    will melt, as mountain-hulk,

marketstalls, kiosks, Cyclopean
    masonry melt
into indigo, into the promise
    hovering above

the harbor. It is not water,
    weed-slung, scummy sloshing, that
survives. It is, in water, the jeweled plummet lines
    of reflected light,

lanterns and neon plunging
    the wavelets' shiver that
establish Night, its dominion
    fathomed in her eyes.

DAILY MAIL

Bare bough clawing out for sky

Street soaring out of town

All the crimped rooftops neatly coiffed
Fences buckle around plump green yards
    buttoned with flagstones

Time wedged in the town hall tower

Sky clamped down
Station closed no trains but tracks still
strike through the heart

and here is the postman again unlocking the trunk
of his car unlocking a day

no sooner read than sentenced

ICE

Lawn a mastodon's matted hide
Roof shingles dinosaur skin

From the fencepost a crow
watches afternoon throttle the small white house

Clouds unskeining from the maple's hands

Down from his front porch
he steps
        the old
man

pauses

Tests
    his balance

on a slab of light

JACOB BURCKHARDT, AUGUST 8, 1897

for C. Vann Woodward

He's dismissed them over
and over: *Gewaltmenschen*, maniacs
of power, like those new *"terribles
simplificateurs* who will descend upon old Europe." But

here they come crowding his room, ghost
shouldering ghost. The window fades
and faces surge, shine
as though lit from within. Good Lord, he is—

he sees it now—he's been
their magic lantern puppeteer
for years, *he's* cast them on
the screen of the world. "To me

history is poetry on the grandest scale." And they have
scale, his people: Alberti, il Moro, blood
in rivulets, poison
globules, dome of domes, "Honor,

that enigmatic mixture of conscience and egoism
surviving the loss of faith, love, hope." He coughs,
wants water, but won't disturb
the nurse asleep in the study.

Ah, but in his loneliness, he's had
love. His kind. Not the young Basel women
with lisps and linens, not widows
longing to dust his books, but

"My fancy is beauty
of spirit. . . . Only ascetics change the world. . . ." Not
plump Emma, cramming the mail
with odes. "Dear Emma,

you must save yourself
from seas of feeling, and reach
art. . . . Not every mood is fit. . . ."
How she will rail! "The golden

shimmer of reconciliation must
hover over the poem. . . ." As over
the deathbed. Aeneas Silvius leans
close, scholar-pope to

scholar-of-popes, and smooths
the sheets across the Professor's chest.
Lorenzo guards the door,
nose whittled white. Dusk throngs

the bedroom with ambassadors,
Luca's cherubs
fingering marble lutes. . . .
The quilt lies heavy, but he can't

lift it: Borgia looms
terror-eyed with poison-sallow skin.
They're closing in
touched with the flames he heard had swept the Louvre

under the Commune, when he wept, and ran
out into his wildering city with the news. They sweep
around the bed, not Silvius, not Lorenzo, but
his more imaginative

freaks, fiery with rings,
vials, sword-hilts, smiles—
Nietzsche among them, loyal
young friend, as Death,

terrible simplificateur,
bends now across the pillow, and shades his eyes.

In Creve Coeur, Missouri

(Pulitzer Prize for photojournalism, 1989)

Only in Creve Coeur
would an amateur photographer
firebug snap a shot so
unconsolable: fireman bent low

over the rag of body held
like impossible laundry pulled
too soon from the line, too pale,
too sodden with smoke to flail

in his huge, dark, crumpled embrace.
He leans to the tiny face.
Her hair stands out like flame.
She is naked, she has no name.

No longer a baby, almost
a child, not yet a ghost,
she presses a doll-like fist
to his professional chest.

Her head falls back to his hand.
Tell us that she will stand
again, quarrel and misbehave.
He is trying to make her breathe.

Strong man, you know how it's done,
you've done it again and again
sucking the spirit back
to us from its lair of smoke.

We'll call it a fine surprise.
The snapshot won a prize
though it couldn't revive *her*
that night in Creve Coeur.

Noon

High summer. Plenitude. The granite knoll
thrusts through gray soil at the hill crest. Drought:
spring is fulfilled. I crouch on the warm skull
of New Hampshire. Spikes of parched grass jut
through the anthill at my feet, and the whole field
grates with small oracles the cicadas
scrape between thigh and wing. What do I hold
at bay? The idea of harvest, days that ooze . . .
From the valley rises the Interstate's purr,
the whine of outboards from the lake, a child's voice
quarreling. Someone's hammer raps the air,
duet with its own knocked echo. Here is the precise
dead heart of the living day, the hollow core, the pit
around which light thickens, and we eat.

Tide pickers

Question marks at the tide line, dark figures bend
to rocks, to kelp, to sighing
pools. They hunt this evening
what they hunted at dawn: what can be kenned

from the ocean's drawl, its lungs
and tongue exposed. The more brutal
question: *will it feed us?* brings
their curled spines an immemorial

conviction. They worry rocks, grapple the sea's
hiss. The sea in its gasping never
answers. Yet centuries
keep lisping the question, and in it whisper another

less pronounceable: *how will we
die?* Phrased and rephrased ad infinitum
and still the sea shrugs off all idiom
and hauls the pickers out as tirelessly

as tides. Figures stalk against the last anemone
glow as Venus rises. Small boats rock
to sleep, Glénan winks from its drowse across the bay,
two figures limned in early moonlight lock:

like the tide pickers against the hollow ocean,
framed in the window, a man and woman bend
down into each other, carving that question
the sea won't answer though human hand grasp hand.

The cormorant

for Eunice

Up through the buttercup meadow the children lead
their father. Behind them, gloom
of spruce and fir, thicket through which they pried
into the golden ruckus of the field, toward home:

this rented house where I wait for their return
and believe the scene eternal. They have been out
studying the economy of the sea. They trudged to earn
sand dollars, crab claws, whelk shells, the huge debt

repaid in smithereens along the shore:
ocean, old blowhard, wheezing in the give
and take, gulls grieving the shattered store.
It is your death I can't believe,

last night, inland, away from us, beyond
these drawling compensations of the moon.
If there's an exchange for you, some kind of bond,
it's past negotiation. You died alone.

Across my desk wash memories of ways
I've tried to hold you: that poem of years ago
starring you in your *mater dolorosa* phase;
or my Sunday picnic sketch in which the show

is stolen by your poised, patrician foot
above whose nakedness the party floats.
No one can hold you now. The point is moot.
I see you standing, marshaling your boats

of gravy, chutney, cranberry, at your vast
harboring Thanksgiving table, fork held aloft
while you survey the victualing of your coast.
We children surged around you, and you laughed.

Downstairs, the screen door slams, and slams me back
into the present, which you do not share.
Our children tumble in, they shake the pack
of sea-treasures out on table, floor, and chair.

But now we tune our clamor to your quiet.
The deacon spruces keep the darkest note
though hawkweed tease us with its saffron riot.
There are some wrecks from which no loose planks float,

nothing the sea gives back. I walked alone
on the beach this morning, watching a cormorant
skid, thudding, into water. It dove down
into that shuddering darkness where we can't

breathe. Impossibly long. Nothing to see.
Nothing but troughs and swells
over and over hollowing out the sea.
And, beyond the cove, the channel bells.

FARM

Once you have described the barn, erase the page.
The wind is sawing the roof off anyway,
it will not stand long. The goat will forage
rose hips on the ridge, and in any case, will die
of hunger and cold come winter. Once you have told
yourself the names of weeds, can distinguish
caraway from deadly water hemlock, hold
the white, lacy blossoms, one in each
hand, and let them spin in the wind. The broken
plank fence divides the meadow from itself
till tawny grass crests over and swallows the line.
The whole shale coastline is sliding off the shelf
into the North Atlantic. Of the couple who lived here once
and quarreled, we know little. Mist deletes the horizon.

III

ALCMAN

FOR JOHN HOLLANDER

They danced to your numbering, to your thumb-
plucked lyre, and shook out long
curls for you, their music master:
around your syllables Hagesichora
and Astymeloisa, loveliest, pressed their lips,
and you noted twilight eyelids, sidelong
glances of the love later called "limb-
loosening" in the dictionaries: all yours,
moved to your measure, in a daze
of buds and petals, stars and feathers,
yours, in Sparta, in the old days
before troops and helots and chariots
protected us from what we might have become.

A GARLAND FROM ALCMAN

I

Desire loosening
arms, knees, thighs, she
 looks at me
 more meltingly
than sleep or death, such
sweetness carries her—

Astymeloisa, swaying
past me, lifts her garland
 high, a star
 skimming the night air,
or green-gold April sprout, or,
softly, a feather

II

They sleep, the mountain crags and gullies,
headlands and brooks, and the whole race
of footed creatures the black earth pulls from its womb,
mountain beasts and the republic of bees,
and vast fish looming in hollows
of purple sea: they sleep,
too, birds with wide, cloud-tipped wings

III

No savage, no boor
or Thessalian lout
you are, no out-
landish shepherd, but
a poet, from high Sardis

An Old Cubist

(Pierre Reverdy photographed by Brassai, Paris, 1947)

He sees your

black look
                    two twinkling glasses of
                    eau-de-vie?
                                        on the
café table

          gentle slouch of overcoat enfolding
          you like a Duccio madonna's

cape
                    How neat
                    severe
          the hat tilted above

                    your brow
                    one eyebrow raised as if some slight

          ironic hope
                              persists
You've paid
Near the coins on the table lie

          a fountain pen
          a small
                    blinding sheet of paper on which

          you haven't written
                    will
                              not write
Angular man
     You won't describe

arabesques smoked in glass on the café door
behind you
                                but your friend
    has trapped you there
At home in the provinces
                        dreary north
    in shadow your melons swell

    At the bottom of a garden
        in a dark hutch
        your white rabbits shuffle and stamp

If you taste a wafer
it will not be sanctified

VERSO

(by Pierre Reverdy)

The room in the draught
Under the flame which spreads
            In the sleeping town
            By moving trees
            Of the stone wall
            At the end of the road
            which circles the earth

                              It's there

head leaning out
      sunbeams near the wave of hair
                  drowned face
                  tears

All the reasons not to believe in anything anymore
Words lost and scattered all along the path
            There's nothing left to say
The wind rises
            The world slips away

                              The other side

SAME TASTE

(by Pierre Reverdy)

Level with my eye the hook's horn from which the
    signboard hangs
        At the end of a longer arm
Let all the windows blaze at the same time
        Let moonlight knock harder against the shutters in
        the street
Let the plaster plaques inscribed with letters fall
        The clock has struck
Water spurted from the chime
        And if someone still hesitates to go back up
            It is not yet time
It is not late enough
                    And for the shadow to die
He remains
Always with this freshness and especially this taste of
    ashes on the tongue and against the night

LOVE IN THE SHOP

(by Pierre Reverdy)

All that's happened slides into half-dark
    It's this ground-floor square which marks the limit and
                              the count

It's a little sunlight
                Hot behind the head
It's a broken glass
    Dust motes or air bubbles rise over
    the screen
Come out on the landing
In the shop love is sold
But this shape of shadow or white or more
    motionless against the drapes
                    In the narrowest corner
                      Who is it

AGONIES AND MORE

(by Max Jacob)

I'm afraid you'll take offense
as I weigh and weigh again
in my works and in my heart
your love from which I live apart
that other love I'm dying in

What will these lines be about
God whom you nag day in day out
God his angels and his priests
or your love's infernal feasts
and their gobbling agonies
Righteous rocks old blood-soaked gods
I leave return veer close again
to my all-too-easy sin
my loves are in my pocket here
I'll sail weeping out to sea

On Edinborough's city wall
so much sorrow marries so
much love
this evening Poetry your horse
wears a black veil

INFERNAL VISION IN THE
FORM OF A MADRIGAL

(by Max Jacob)

"Handsome knights of Alcantara
Venus of Marnes-la-Coquette
The nabob of Calatrara
Offers you his private yacht
to sail away to Guatemala."

When I had renounced your love, oh women,
when I had of pleasure intoned the requiem
    and conquered Bethlehem

When I had cast off the henbane of this world
And of the Wandering Jew's eternal
    voyage the sail unfurled

When, beneath the cramped balcony, the vice
squad and its laughter ringing de profundis
    knocking as in the old days
at my door to enroll me in its militias
I had made my room a secret oasis
    or almshouse

I did not yet know the clear sky of your eyes
the snowy kingdom of your limbs in summer
nor the perfumed hell in your thick hair
nor your beauty which will by my Holy Grail
nor your soul for which I shall be Parsifal.

"Handsome knights of Alcantara
Handsome knights of Alcantara
all aboard! anchors aweigh!

—Let them rush off toward the tropics,
I have only one mystic exodus
one reliquary and its relic
I have one tender oasis only: you,
your eyes, their forget-me-not blue."

CHRIST AT THE MOVIES

(by Max Jacob)

"When you're eating fruit, child, spit the seeds out,
Or in your little belly a whole tree will sprout,"
They said in my house when I was a boy.
That set me on the wrong track for sure:
Branches in the navel mean fruit all the more.
A tree all my own which no one takes away,
Whose fruit, no sooner eaten, grows back every day!

I have my tree today: my tree is the Cross;
Faith is its gift to my greediness.
Dryad of the gallows, when I summon you, come:
Rescue my life from its cruel humdrum.
Dryad of the gallows, descend like yesterday
Evening at the movies when you sat by me
So close. Your hand! Put your hand upon mine
And your so-human warmth and your breath divine.
Oh! I was sick and tired from thinking too much.
Let my body fold upon yours at your touch.
And you! You deigned, as your shoulder hid my eyes,
To describe the movie and sort out the lines.
We had the cheapest seats, at ninety-five centimes;
You spoke of charity before those murky crimes
The Parisian wants every night for dessert.
Today, I'm alone. Lord, groping at my side
My eager fingers feel only the void.
Without you, my God, the world is blank, inert.
The eyes of my spirit sketch your body still,
But it's mere imagination, an act of the will.
—When I go lug my spleen through Montparnasse
Do you want me to save a place in the cafés
For this body you give so generously
To the humblest, most useless, of servants: to me?

That idiot movie! Now I find it blessed.
Since you deigned, so my faith would be redressed,
To sit at my side amidst your people there.
A movie seat held you! It is a holy chair!

They call me crazy! Yes! I hear the reader now—
Or blasphemous, you scold with furrowed brow.
Madmen yourselves, if truth can make you laugh.
The Lord is everywhere, and with the worst riffraff.
To feel God in oneself, to hear Him, to reply,
Whether at the movies, in the street, at a café,
This common miracle shouldn't start a fuss:
Outside of church, God's everywhere, and speaks with us.
My madness, if I'm mad, is of a different brand.
Listen: I've seen Him! Twice, close at hand:
It was October seven, rue Ravignan, in my room—
No! I wasn't drunk, nor in delirium—
In the year nineteen-oh-nine, October seven;
I take you as witness, Lord, who put new leaven
Into me, sinning lump of filthiness;
You know what sins had seized me in their fists,
What hell I lived in, what a squalid mess,
What resolutions you raised up like yeast
In this Christian whom, thanks to you and the good priests,
I've become, endowed with sense and reason.
So, the first time, you appeared in my room.
And the second time, it was at a film.
"You go to the movies, then?" with dumbfounded air
Demanded my confessor.—Yes, Father,
What if I did? Didn't Our Lord go there?"

"The Gang in the Black Suits," thriller by Paul Féval;
The plot's in my heart and not on the screen.
The cops and mounties close round and corral
A thief in dire straits: a sudden sheen
Spreads over the crowd, my eyes fill with tears!
The sheen is a halo, in its light, God appears.

To me, this gift! Why did you choose to meet
Me here? In this movie on a little side street
The drapes of a taper-white mantle enfold
My concierge's four urchins you once told
Me to care for. Can the human soul
Hide no scrap from your eyes, must it be seen whole?
Is there for your vision no mystery in our heart?
Do you penetrate all beings in every part?
Then why? Why this grace
If you know my life in all its ugliness?
If you know my faults and my weaknesses too?
What in me, oh Lord, could interest you?

IV

Necrophiliac

More marrow to suck, more elegies
to whistle through the digestive track. So help
me God to another dollop of death,
come on strong with the gravy and black-eyed peas,
slop it all in the transcendental stew
whose vapors rise and shine in the nostrils of heaven.
Distill the belches, preserve the drool as ink:
Death, since you nourish me, I'll flatter you
inordinately. Consumers both, with claws
cocked and molars prompt at the fresh-dug grave,
reaper and elegist, we collaborate
and batten in this strictest of intimacies,
my throat an open sepulchre, my tongue
forever groping grief forever young.

His long home

FOR RPW, 1905–1989

I

Of Course

From lips notched in the pinebranch bled
no confession, but a clot of resin.
Such currency
in winter. No need to notch

the stream, ice-choked but still
greenly slurring
past boulders and scragwood to some ever-lapsing
period not even January

can grant. If you and I
stand, in silence, to observe
that pregnant snowcloud stalled
on Stratton's frozen stoop

it is in the knowledge
that what courses between us, runs
under the rind of winter
so deep, no blade can coax it.

II

Storm, Summer

At first a numbness
gaining on the surface of the pond,
a twitching in birch and poplar leaves,
tremor in the flat, symmetrical branchtips of balsalm pine.
Then thunder surges, thudding from ridge to ridge,
a seizure of rain

sunders spiderwebs, pummels leafmold,
drowns out the true confessions of the brook.
While we cower on the porch
it passes
like a spasm,
heaves itself into the valley
over the notch.
Sky shimmers in the pond again,
breeze fondles the leaves.
We're still here. Waiting.

III

Your skin

as fragile, pale, and infinitesimally moist
as erasable bond;
your look, a startled bound
of apprehension, subsiding
into its lair.
You coil away from us:
we hunt you down.
Groping, you half-rise:
we escape, leave you there.
What intersections can we appoint
between your knowledge
and ours?

IV

Two days before

you died, we saw your death
funneling in at the eye, your pupil fixed,
tiny, waking neither
to light nor to shade

so that your wisdom drained
inward where only
reverberations of our
voices fathomed:

yet you held us still
kindly, having foreknown
the sere flame tasseling
the roof beam, the palace wall

sinking but invisible
to the chorus; and in the teeth
of our denial
had already greeted

the strange man you alone
saw loitering by the porch,
had wrenched up your
emaciated smile: "Come in! Come in!"

Song

A yellow coverlet
in the greenwood:
spread the corners wide to the dim, stoop-shouldered pines.
Let blank sky
be your canopy.
Fringe the bedspread with the wall of lapsing stones.
Here faith has cut
in upright granite
"Meet me in Heaven" at the grave of each child
lost the same year,
three, buried here,
a century ago. Roots and mosses hold
in the same bed
mother, daughter, dead
together, in one day. "Lord, remember the poor,"
their crumbling letters pray.
I turn away.
I shall meet you nowhere, in no transfigured hour.
On soft, matted soil
blueberry bushes crawl,
each separate berry a small, hot globe of tinctured sun.
Crushed on the tongue
it releases a pang
of flesh. Tender flesh, slipped from its skin,
preserves its blue heat
down my throat.

Man, that is born of a woman

It is in slow choking
that leaves flare.
And that single spider strand
flung between shrubs
catches nothing but sun splinters.
Each leaf an hour.
Look, look, the hours
shudder against the regulation blue.
Warm palm on granite:
it's only my own
pulse cantering
as it did against your
cold and stiffening hand.
All around me, life
grips: the oak leaf stem
holds hard the throttling twig,
lichen and moss seize
the Precambrian ledge, wild
grapevines strangle
the beech: my
hand, gripping
this granite glacial
shelf, could clench as surely
an alto-cirrus wisp,
as freely
let it go.

From new hampshire

It's not your mountain
but I almost expect
to meet you here

I think you have taken a long late evening walk
Your heavy shoes glisten with dew
I hear your footsteps pause on the dirt road

and I know you are picking out
the dark mass of the sleeping
mountain from the dark

mass of night and testing the heaviness of each
Your hands are small but they know weights and measures
You are a connoisseur of boundaries

You loved the bears
because they pass between
leaving their stories

in fat pudding turds on the grass
Here it's raspberries they're after not our
sour Vermont apples   No matter   You will find them

When they hoot in courtship
you always hoot back
more owl than bear

They don't mind   They always answer you
And tonight I imagine you're out waiting up for them
by the berries, which is why you don't cross

the dew-sopped lawn
don't press open the
warped screen door

of the kitchen where I sit late   by a single glowing bulb

MOUNTAIN VIEW

(Franconia, New Hampshire)

Evening pulls a counterpane of shadow over Lafayette
outlining vertebrae, steep shoulder blades, groin,
and clustered here at the porch, tiger lilies and lupin
squeeze petals softly inward, enclosing twilight.

Last bird twitters fringe the meadow. I am alone
drawing the hour slowly around my shoulders,
hugging hunger as dusk drifts down and bewilders
the notebook page, its school-careful lines, the pen

motionless now as I pause and watch a biplane
hoist a glider into the virtual sky.
From the house down the road rises a child's cry.
The plane and its charge pass out of my field of vision,

they will release one another soon into high air.
It will be dark for the glider, lofted on weightlessness,
free to inscribe a line which leaves no trace,
floating toward nightfall, out of otherwhere.

LENA'S HOUSE:
WATERCOLOR

for ECW, with apologies to Sir Philip Sidney

To have come so far into this sodden green
was an adjustment of perspective, a division
of space, as through window bars, so the middle distance
of Lena's house, the curving road, alders and hill
would reveal themselves in diptych and not lose
ground by settling back into mere landscape:

since that is what we were after, a promise of landscape
raw beyond the familiar, a quickened green,
a new kinship system of colors in which to lose
our brushes. How else measure the division
between the hills of childhood and this further hill
we seem always to be scaling, into a distance

ever lonelier, more blurred? It is not distance
we're after, but clarity. One of the uses of landscape
is to stand for something else. Otherwise the hill
merely spills down across the retinal green
and mere displacement in space gives no division.
To have come so far: there was the risk we'd lose

track of the subject, which is "the child's reluctance to
                                              lose
the mother." Yes, the bifocal study of distance
displaces into pigment the pang of division
and stirs up turmoil in a peaceful landscape
as Prussian blue beslobbers the muted green
of Lena's lawn. Watercolor dissolves the hill

Into a lowe dejected vallie, though Lena's hill
framed in the window looks hardly likely to lose

status in the gravitational world when I squint from the
green
Pontine marsh on my paper out into the distance.
That is another consolation of landscape:
you rip off the page, you start a new division

of shapes and spaces, whereas the human division
scars forever. "Is gone, is gone," each hill
and spoilèd forrest echoes, and no escape
beckons. In my nightmare, I thought I'd lose
her who had given me first the gift of distance,
I thought in coming away I'd blight all green

forever. Hardly. Tears are the source of vision
whose lens dilates to embrace the original hill
and compose in every scene the maternal landscape.

THE BROKEN POT

FOR ECW

The Mother is present in every house. Need I break the news as one breaks an earthen pot on the floor? Ramprāsād (1718–1775)

I

I am far from you, I am walking farther
down the peninsular road in a borrowed landscape.
From the soggy meadow, a red cow and her calf
observe me, and go on munching. They are densely matted
with rain. They stand their ground. Raindrops bedeck
the rusty tractor parked at the edge of the field,
the barbed wire, the arcing boughs of wintergreen
weighted down with garnet berries.
At the far rim of the field, skeletal oaks
and birches stalk the shore of a tidal inlet
and I stride on, through drizzle, down the road
to the summer cottages in their winter autism,
to the last spine of rock dragged bare by the tide.
There, at the farthest verge, the open sea
is merely an intuition through shawled mist.

The road loops back. Evening closes in,
I let the road have its way and lead me home.
By now, the cow and her calf must be in the barn.
Their meadow lies open in the seeping light.
I am absentminded. But the cattle,
standing quietly together, had shaped the field,
and shape it still in their absence, breathing
together in the ruminant, gaseous dark
where I cannot see them.

II

Your Christmas narcissi, too leggy for their frills,
pitched from your table.
You had thought the bulbs were onions, kept them
refrigerated in the vegetable drawer
and narrowly missed a very bitter stew.
You are alone in your rooms
where the Braque bird spreads broad wings
over your past, sheltering in his flight
so many losses
               that your thinness now
seems the very principle of subtraction
as if light were carving you away before our eyes.

III

And Rome rises
in your mind, ruinous and fecund
as in your girlfriend when you foresaw,
looking back.

in its columns, arches, esplanades,
processions, prisoners, imperial gore
the fountain jet
of all our human life, that glittering arc:

foresaw
piazzas, domes, receding colonnades
scooped out of solitude

the internal city
a habitable beauty
subsisting on disappearance

monument to which I turn now
with my tribute
of broken shards, my *symbolon*

from the original vessel in whose clay we share.

UMBILICAL

for KATHERINE, AGE EIGHT

It is not the first time
I have lost you,
betrayed you to the air:

your first cry
was witness enough.
Now you are goat-limbed,

shadow-eyed, and they wheel
you in fluorescent
silence down

a lengthening hall.
Neither of us protests.
You are swathed in sheets,

your body too long
and angular
to have curled in mine.

I let you fall
into the hands
of strangers, you grow

beyond me. In the waiting
room, I devour
a sandwich of

something limp, warm;
an article on
adoption; Balzac's

arias of debit
and credit. All time
sucks into void until

you land in time
stunned on the
recovery room bed.

How touch your other-
worldly skin? Blood drools
from your nostrils.

As your lids
quaver open and
pain hits, two

slow rivulets brim
and trek: from outer
space, you watch me.

Balzac thought money
wrenched the human
bond. It is our own

gravity draws us
down. I have
fallen light years

from my mother's
touch, yet now across
the waste of sheets

you ask me, "Hold
my hand." We are
in reach: and palm

to palm our life-
lines trace, for a
moment, a map.

THE TWELFTH DAY

for Pam Cantor

It is the twelfth day
The hero will not take food
He refuses wine   sleep   women

How can the body not spoil?
Dragged by chariot
gashed   smeared

in mud and horse droppings
Mutilate Mutilate
cries the hero's heart

as he lashes the horses
around and
around the tomb

If he can just
make his mark on this
corpse whose

beauty freshens
with each lunge
as though bathed

in balm   Even the gods
in gentle feast are
shocked: Is there no

shame? The hero has
no other life
He has taken

to heart a body
whose face vaulting
through gravel and blood

blends strangely
with the features
of that other

one: the Beloved
For this is
love: rigor

mortis in the
mortal grip
and never to let

go Achilles hoards
and defiles the dead
So what if heaven

and earth reverberate
release   So what
if Olympian

messages shoot through
cloudbanks sea
chambers ether

So what if everything
echoes the Father   *let go let*
go   This is Ancient

Poetry   It's supposed
to repeat
The living mangle the dead

after they mangle the living
It's formulaic
That's how we love   It's called

compulsion   Poetry can't
help itself
And no one has ever

explained how
light stabbed
the hero how he saw

in dawn salt mist
his Mother's face (she who
Was before words she

who would lose him)
Saw her but heard
words *Let him let*

go   Saw her and let
his fingers loosen
from that

suspended decay and
quietly
too quietly

turned away

NOTES

"Eskimo Widow" and "Eskimo Mother": I am indebted to Robin Hansen for her translation from the Danish of Kirsten Bang's *Ande manerens Larling* (*The Shaman's Apprentice*: Nyt Nordisk Forlag/ Arnold Busck, 1967) accounts of life among the Angmagssalikmiut people of eastern Greenland.

"Science Lessons": The man in question is John Wilmot, Earl of Rochester.

"Jacob Burckhardt, August 8, 1897": The great Swiss historian of culture lectured at the University of Basel, his native city, on and off from 1843 to 1893. Friedrich Nietzsche held the chair of classical philology at Basel from 1869–1879, and saw a good deal of Burckhardt, whom he revered. Later, during a breakdown, Nietzssche wrote a postcard to Burckhardt, saying that if he were not already God, the next best thing would be to be Professor Burckhardt ("signed, Dionysus"). The fantasies in the poem are culled, of course, from Burckhardt's *The Civilization of the Renaissance in Italy*. The quotations come from Burckhardt's letters.

"Alcman": Alcman was a choral poet who composed in Sparta in the second half of the 7th century B.C.E. He is rumored to have come from Sardis. Sparta did not take on its grim, militaristic character until two centuries later.

"An Old Cubist": Born in Narbonne in the South of France, Pierre Reverdy moved to Paris in 1910 and joined the group of artists and poets around Picasso at the Bateau Lavoir in Montmartre. An austere and haunting writer, he published many books of poems and some art criticism, and founded the important avant-garde journal *Nord-Sud* (1917–1919). He died at Solesmes, where he had retreated at the time of his conversion to Roman Catholicism. He had distanced himself from the Church by the time of his death.

Max Jacob (1876–1944). A Breton Jew, Max Jacob went to Paris for his studies in 1894, and around 1903 joined Picasso, Apollinaire, and André Salmon to form the nucleus of the Cubist group at the Bateau Lavoir. After a mystical vision, Jacob converted to Roman Catholicism, and was baptized in 1915 with Picasso as his godfather. From 1921–1928 and from 1937–1944, he lived in retreat at the Benedictine monastery of Saint-Benoît-sur-Loire, where he continued to write poetry and fiction, and to paint the gouaches he sold for a living. He died of pneumonia (from exposure and ill treatment) at the French Nazi camp at Drancy, March 5, 1944.